Dog Island

and Other Florida Poems

Shrimp Boats at Carrabelle

Dog Island

and Other Florida Poems

Laurence Donovan

Pineapple Press, Inc. Sarasota, Florida

Inquiries should be addressed to:

Pineapple Press, Inc.
P.O. Box 3889
Sarasota, Florida 34230
www.pineapplepress.com

Library of Congress Cataloging-in-Publication Data
Donovan, Laurence, 1927–
     Dog Island and other Florida poems / by Laurence Donovan— 1st ed.
     p. cm.
     ISBN 1-56164-284-3 (hardback. : alk. paper)
     1. Florida—Poetry. 2. Islands—Poetry. I. Title.

PS3604.O567 D64 2003
811'.54—dc21

                                                                 2003011003

First Edition
10 9 8 7 6 5 4 3 2 1

Design by Shé Heaton
Printed in the United States of America

Contents

Dune Pine

Foreword
by Donald Justice

. . . high sand dunes covered with scrubby pines, sea oats, and white sand. Wide stretches of salt meadows are feeding grounds of herons and other wading birds. Long piers jut out from shore, and mounds of oystershells surround the weathered frame shacks of the fishermen. . . .
—The American Guide Series 1939

Laurence Donovan, poet and graphic artist, was born in Vancouver, British Columbia, January 17, 1927. His father was a writer of pulp fiction and radio drama. One tale has it that Mr. Donovan was offered the job of preparing the script for the silent-screen version of *Ben Hur,* but blew his chances by going off, at just the wrong time, on one of his binges. The family moved across country from place to place including Connecticut and ending in Florida. By the time Larry was ten, the family was breaking up, and the mother moved, with her two sons, Larry and his younger brother, Pat, to Miami. From then until his death at seventy-four (July 27, 2001), Larry lived in Miami, seldom leaving it except for a period at the University of Iowa Writers Workshop. For more than thirty years he taught literary courses, many of his own devising, at the University of Miami, from which he had graduated.

Despite his formidable skills as a printmaker, it was literature he taught rather than art. He was one of the "doubly gifted." He liked to say the poets thought his art was great and the artists thought his poetry was great. I knew him first as a young poet like myself, and only later as the master printmaker he was to become. Whether he had been quietly practicing, almost in secret, the art of drawing, which was to lead to the late and very beautiful etchings of Dog Island gathered here, I never thought to ask. I do have a vague and uncertain memory of being shown casually one afternoon a large and elaborate ink drawing that must have taken, even at Larry's great speed, many hours of devoted labor, rendered, as it was, in obsessive detail and a variety of colors. If it looked at all familiar, that was probably because it brought to mind some of the cartoons he had contributed to university humor magazines while still a student. But on the whole it looked most like an illustration for some untold story, possibly meant for children. Its geniality and good humor, its freedom from all pretension, its simple pleasure in itself—all these seemed packed together, present from the beginning. Thus a stray memory: I had not realized until now how lasting an impression this early drawing would make. There would be many fantasy scenes like this one over the years—a world of his own building up around the artist, the half-hidden ambition behind the work only gradually coming into focus, even for the friends who had loved his work from the start.

Graphics were his specialty. Painting he scarcely tried, despite the urging of his friends. He talked about "the clean line"; liked Blake, Munch, and the German Expressionists; hated abstraction and what he termed "fuzzy"; and preferred work that had not been "fooled around with." Baskin and Gropper were on his walls. And of course these preferences and leanings showed up in his own work, set against the trends and fashions of the time and place. His defiant taste must have had something to do with the solitariness of his fame, but I never got the impression that he thought he was wrong. His work was shown in small galleries in and around Miami, occasionally elsewhere; and in the sixties, when for a brief period Coconut Grove became the local center for new art, Larry himself kept a small upstairs gallery there until the rent was jacked up too high for the kind of art Larry cared for. Before that there had been the clothesline sales on weekends, a sociable custom of which Larry was one of the stars. But the walls of doctors' offices and Grove living rooms were too soon filled. For some years he worked mostly for himself. For a certain type of artist that is no doubt the best way to go about it. Larry was of that type.

To be doubly gifted, as Larry was, is a rare thing, though not perhaps as rare as one supposes. After all, there was Blake, there was Strindberg; there were e.e. cummings and D.H. Lawrence, Weldon Kees, and Marsden Hartley as well as in more recent history, Henry Miller, Fairfield Porter, A. R. Ammons, Elizabeth Bishop, Derek Walcott, and Mark Strand; these, among many others; and in all cases, it seems, one side of his work is better known, valued more highly. This is true of Donovan's double labors as well, for it is impossible, for me, at least, to think of his poetry without thinking first of his graphics. Nevertheless, one senses the constant pull of poetry that underlies his art. This hovering, vague sense shows itself most clearly, of course, in an actual poem such as the long poem which accompanies the *Dog Island* etchings.

Unless I am mistaken, "Dog Island" is his longest and most ambitious poem. (It is scarcely shorter than "the Waste Land.") I believe it is also his best. In the late forties and early fifties a sort of school of young poets had a brief flourishing in Miami—Ronald Perry, Larry himself, perhaps Robert Boardman Vaughn, and a few others I have by now forgotten. These poets were touched by Stevens, Dylan Thomas, and Hart Crane, but most of all by one another, as is usually the case in such matters. I think it is still possible to see the school-like character of their poems in "Dog Island," though it was written decades later. These Miami poets had been understandably taken by the beauty of the place, which managed to remain, at least for the purposes of art, semi-primitive a surprisingly long time while all around them a very new metropolis was growing up. Now it was more likely a place of refuge the artist might feel the need of, an escape. For Larry Dog Island seems to have been that. Larry visited it twice, in 1979 and 1987, in company with Dee Clark, a fellow artist, whose brother has a vacation home on the island. Larry had always been partial to trees like the banyan and the mangrove, the grotesque and the exotic. Now the "twisted" dune pine was added. His

11

treatment of subject in the *Dog Island* series is more naturalistic than usual—rich in detail, but natural, yes, and without embellishment. The Dune Pine becomes so enwrapped in its own detail that it approaches fantasy; it becomes emblematic, almost dreamlike. There is some meaning here, but what is it? It is hidden from us, in part by the very technique which sponsored a certain air of mystery in the first place, of humble awe. If I were to speculate further along these lines, it would be to suggest that the whole sequence, by chance if by nothing else, evokes the earthly paradise, with the dune pine at the symbolic center. And what of the serpent? As for the human pair who sketch together in isolation from the other (the real) world, are they not the Adam and Eve of this landscape? The poet does not insist on interpretation, but it is there for those who want it.

The last twenty years of Larry Donovan's life were beset by various illnesses, especially diabetes; in 1992 he had triple-bypass surgery; toward the end he was taking eleven different medications. But in spite of his health problems he managed to do an impressive body of work. (Art works left at his death numbered around 2500. Books in his library, around 7000.) He had eventually to undergo a corneal transplant. Working on the etchings for this book, he had the bad luck to fall and damage the transplant, whereupon he was rushed to a hospital emergency room, luckily saving the eye.

His vision was coming along fine when his heart gave out.

—Donald Justice, 2003

The editor has selected a few earlier Florida poems and graphic works the author had sent from a bounty of them to publish along with "Dog Island."

Dog Island

I

Coming out from Carrabelle

South through the veering channel

Into Saint George Sound,

Past the weathered docks and sheds

Of the fishery with its pungent near-rot

Of salt and fish odors, and the unaccustomed

Stinging spray and hollow slap

Of the pummeled hull, sunglare

A white maze over the whipping awning,

I crouch, palest of landsmen,

Amid the strewn tackle and groceries,

Skull grinning into the wind.

Ferry Pier, Dog Island

Pelicans hunch on their perches

Like old men remembering, and

Gulls swing distantly into the sky.

Shapely and neat in their tangle

Of masts and fulcrumed V's and baled

Nets the shrimpers are berthed

In their postures of pure labor

Beside the poisoned sea.

The water rolls gray underneath

The light chop, from which our wake

Unravels, bubbling its skein outward

From that less-trafficked coast

Toward a finer diminishment.

As St. Thomas or Cap Haitien once

17

Threaded the far horizon

In the tourist's eye, as the tiny isle

Of pines off the Grove marina

Piratically dissolved the mainland,

On the blind side eclipsing

Its lights in the murmuring sea,

Or as the Apalachicola, draining

Down history, once slowly silted

Her three barrier islands

Up from the crystal and coral,

Up from the stormshoals

Hung with the ravenous fish,

So there seems now out of loss

Some kingly issuance or release, an

Old dream of solar and sea desire:

It is perhaps that blue voyage

At last, as the plunging launch

Divides the long sealane

With its silver finger,

Buffeted down it

Into the sea and the rising

Island beyond. . . .

II

Were the French in 1536

Plagued by wild dogs

Or had the whole island assumed

In dazzled voyagers' eyes

A vast canine shape

Athwart the blue delta?

Or had they only dumped

Their dog sailors there

So they wouldn't jump ship

On the beckoning coast?

However it was

All rumor of dog

Coming down through time

Was reduced for me,

One shimmering, blowing,

Cigar-smoking morning,

In a solitary

Domestic specimen—

Some kind of terrier

With collar and tag—

That slowly picked

Its way in my eyes

Down the long path

From the road

Through the dunes,

Sniffing about

In the sand and the gorse,

Like any mainlander

In neighboring yards.

Dog Island I

When I arose

To look down on him

From my high balcony,

He fled whimpering up the path,

Apprehensive as I, I suppose,

Of the island's small terrors,

The odd desolation

Of a place without sidewalks,

Where the human presence

Looms like a ghost.

III

Smalldroning through the sky

Light craft of all sorts

Can over the shoreline,

Ranging the length

Of the eight-mile island,

Scanning sharkshadows

And chevrons of foam:

They soar at their ease

Among Dog Island birds.

Loon, grebe and cormorant,

Pelican, heron,

Teal, hawk and woodchuck,

Bittern and widgeon,

Turnstone and plover,

Pintail and skinner,

Kestrel and merlin

Afloat in the seawinds.

24

Beyond the landing

Where we disembarked,

Near the junk-row

Of rusted-out vehicles

Undone by the sun

And salt and bad roads,

The small planes are moored.

They appear light as the wind

Which will take them up,

Buzzing like toys, among

Vulture and eagle,

Four kinds of egret,

Ibis and osprey,

Rail, tern and piper,

Dove, cuckoo, sparrow,

Scissored flycatcher,

And most frequent of all

The willet and grackle,

Whose small feathers widen

In our long glasses.

IV

By day the quick willets

Print the moment

In the sluiced-over sand.

On pipecleaner legs

They peck at surf's edge,

Withdrawing and advancing

With the waves' erasures.

Dimmer white against white,

Their pale negative's

An old sketch of creation.

By night the grackles come down

For the crumbs we put out

On the balcony railing.

They approach from afar

In cartoonish transitions,

Hopping nearer and nearer

Through the soughing pines

To the final dark swoop

And quick flight away,

Crumbs dripping from beak.

The males are grand,

Although shifty and baleful,

And even sardonic

With that one beady eye

(Taken from Poe)

That is meant to transfix:

They hide in near branches,

Their black silhouettes

Cut in black arcs.

The females are smaller,

Quicker, less fearful,

And impatient to feed:

They come in for the crumbs,

Hop and peck, hop and peck,

In fluttery incisive

Stabs from the air,

Scratching swift glyphs,

Humorous inkings,

Against the lineage,

Pale, of the pines.

V

Scorpion in the shoe,

Thornbush scratches,

Pines on Dog Island

Snake in the crabtrap,

Airconditioners

Pumping rusty

Against the old sun.

And once in a while

The sonic crack

Of killer birds

Out of Texas

Splitting the sky,

Jarring the

Grey, splotched,

Rotten-grained wood,

Drained of all

But essential color,

Nail-slatted by hand,

Forming

Small pale rotundas,

Or hexagonal

Primitive forts

On the stilts which grow

From the sand shifting

Against the sea:

Here, facing the sea's

Empty expanse, its

Vast dream of water,

The long past reemerges,

Once known by a boy

On a grove isle,

Where the ancient

Oncoming waves

Or the winds of the storm

Flowed through the heart,

And the lights of man

Blinked only dimly

Under the moon:

On Dog Island at night

The lit beach is eerie,

Bleached like a tintype,

Spiked with its tangles

Of shrubbed sea and salt,

Straining the ages

In its ghostly web,

With the sea's constant voice

Out of the darkness,

And the aura of dream

In its luminous sand.

VI

1

In the island's white light,

Out of clump of palmetto

Night Beach on Dog Island

Bur and sandscrub,

Thin patches of seagorse,

And meadowy salt-reed

Waving the wind,

Just down from the hutch

Where we lived that summer,

The dune pine twisted.

From where we sat

It just barely lifted

Its stars of needles

To horizon level,

Its blown, bent limbs

Crowding the squares

Of our drawings,

Much as it clung

In its own hot air

To the treacherous sand

Against sea's ravages,

Pulled down and inward

By insistent margins.

Daily in the shade

Of the stilted house,

We drew that squat pine,

With squint eyes and wet wrists,

Inking slowly

Its intricate coilings,

Dog Island Retreat

Tracing lines of weather

In the wind-wrinkled bark,

Watching it grow

In its crouch on our pages,

Our fisted fingers

Tendrilling the sand.

Then in late afternoon

We'd walk up the dunes,

Our eyes narrowed

To the sprays of sand

In the flaying wind

To swim in the sea.

Once, out beyond the breakers,

Dog Island VIII

The wing of a ray

Brought us, tumbling, to shore.

2

So here now are the etchings

Made from those drawings,

That dune pine

More grandly contained

In the cramp of the burin,

More sieged by the wind

And the salt and the sea,

Gnarled to the bone

Of those burning days.

VII

The island's dark reminders

Could be simple and direct:

Coming in once from a swim

To rinse off in the trickling

Shower under the hutch,

In the cool pentagon of shadows

Beneath, with its chopping board

And scales glued in fish slime

And clutter of cork and net,

And the rusted hanging pipe

With skewed nozzle overhead,

My body hot from the long walk

Through the dragging sand,

And somewhat blinded now

In out of the light, I tossed

My towel on a nearby crabtrap:

In which, freezing me there,

The undulant, velvety, inconceivable

Figure of a water moccasin,

Its lidded eyes seizing mine

And its forked tongue flicking,

Waited on its coils

Inches from my hand.

VIII

The click-hum of the frogs wells up in the pond

Down toward the sea from our hutch, then subsides,

Then swells again, and on and on, in a round

Of croaking and humming that brings the evening,

Once ours in silence, its implacable voice,

Speaking in and of itself, wholly leavening

Our presence here, much as the tides

Of day remind us, in their endless turning,

Sharp slaps and diminishing whispers, that we

Are but interlopers:

                              throbbing frogthroats rehearse

What is ancient and wordless, far beyond

The sails and the footprints, an old song spinning

Over and over, over and over, out of the pond

Through the pines and then out to sea.

Window on Dog Island

IX

Jolting down the shell-tamped dirt road

In golf-cart or jalopy, with their rusted-

Out and salt-bitten, cracked-paint exteriors,

Past the platformed spidering beach house

Of the famous golf-pro, whose manicured greens

Have dwindled here into a barbarous

Opposite, not velveteen cupping its tidy traps

But gorse and barbed thicket and dune pine

Seizing against the wind the long patches

Of sand; past the single double-decked inn

And the garbage dump under its thrumming flies,

Down the slowcurving spine of the island

Dog Island IX

To the swampy woods at the western end

Where St. George lies hazy on the far horizon;

Or walking in the sand, eyes out for snakes,

On road- or beach-side of swept-up dunes,

Combed smooth or crumbling in sea and wind,

With long filaments of stubbled vine fingering down

To moist clumps of seaweed lying in lines

Parallel to the water: eyes down or drawn out to

The Gulf under its eye-dazzling sky, pale

Blue or blindingly white as sheet metal; past

Remnants of pierwalks, lines of descending

Stakes in the sand, rotting wooden markers

Whose decks have flown into the whorls of the storm;

Walking like Crusoe on his old island,

Hushed in that monotone, the surf's sibilant whisper,

The curlew's soundless patter, the shellpop underfoot.

X

Beginning far out

Beyond the eye's fathoming,

From somewhere over the hairline edge

That separates sea and sky, mounting and mounting

Out of cumbrous depths its dark humpings of water,

In a thunderous drumming, the sea rolls in, rolls in

All along the coast, each redundant wave flowing

Forth from another, in wide, sweeping ranks,

With chevroning, crisscrossing lines of white lace,

Rising up, and up, in an ultimate towering, to suddenly

Crumble, spill over, and slide, in great hissings of foam,

Up the whispering beach, in near retrograde motion,

In diminishing scrolls, in that indwelling pause

At the point of reversal,

        where it suavely pivots

And falls back again, smoothing out its long skirts

Of receding water, sucking tumbling shells down

Through the puckering sand,

To render the incoming

Tide of itself.

XI

Eyes dissolving in sealight,

I watch the waves thinly lacing—

After each mild boom and crest—

The imprinted sand at my feet,

Scattering the quick willets,

And then, receding from them,

Drawing them back to the rim.

Standing at this last portal,

Turned from where I'll return to—

The long channel, the drumming

Roads south—I watch the sea

Spread to its own horizon,

Lending grey washes of color

To hollow, white arches of sky

And in its empty vastness,

Through attenuations of light,

Draw me into that vastness.

Perhaps all I'll ever know

Remains at last in this light

Borne on the incoming waves

Into the beach's deep silence.

Here where the Union navy

Plucked those barrier islands

From under rebel eyes

And boats of Sparta and Thebes

(My reading up in the hutch)

Shed their old blood in the sea,

And that stain washed away in the sea

And the sea remained as before;
Here where a carpetbagger
Promised men he'd farm oysters
But farmed only their pockets,
And the exiled Apalachees
Drifted from Spanish eyes—
I watch the long coiling waves

Advancing out of their dream,
Breaking onto Dog Island,
Erasing for swift renewal
The messages the willets

Leave in the puckering sand,

And I see sketched emblems of gulls

Lift in the vanishing light. . . .

Etching the
Sea Grape Tree

Crouched in the unrelenting heat

of the tropical day,

situated in the only place of vantage

from which I can trace

the front-yard sea grape tree,

encompass its indolent, intricate sprawl

across the hot zinc plate in my lap,

sweat drips

in beads on the brown surface,

and I'm fearful the willful sun

will puddle the wax,

Sea Grape

muddy my own eyes' tight designs,

and spread, with the acid's terminal assistance,

surrealist blooms,

a solar ghost-tree in the air,

neither mine nor the tree's

ineluctable image.

Finger and eye and wrist narrowed

to the burin's taut

dipping and weaving, I scratch

hentracks of veins, doodle

enclosing hearts around the arrowing

parallel

silver flecks, my thumb

sweeping the fine trough's displaced

waxdust away,

drawing leaf from leaf, leaf

upon leaf, among grapelike clusters

of tiny berries,

then twigs into branches, beginning and lengthening

and joining, the tree shaping slowly

across the plate's top

in a tangled yet wavelike accretion

of parts. I pause only

to cool the plate with a cloth

and, blinking and wiping the sweat

from my eyes, survey anew

through framing fingers

the tree's gathered presence, so imperial

on the suburban lawn. Then I begin again,

clenched hand

in contention with the wrist's limpid flow,

tracing and tracing the fanned-out form

(though seen only now

as a silvery web in the burning wax)

of the sea-blown tree, spirited from the sea

to this inland perch

among the domestic pine and the mango.

The earth turns gradually

toward dusk and a cooling wind ripples

through the paddle-shaped leaves: I bend

at the last to etch in the trunk, growing

amazingly

downward out of the floating branch and leafcrest,

as if in some strange reversal the tree

were seeking

from out of the sky its rock-soil

to root in, in the same way its image flows

down from my eyes

into my wrist and my hand and my fingers:

and the drawing is finished. Now, later,

in the nitric bath,

its mazed lines erupting in a tinsel

of silver bubbles,

in a fiercer heat than that of the sun,

the sea grape grows and deepens, until,

its waxen envelope washed away,

it is inked

and cradled and cooled in blankets and blotters,

and pressed into paper, its new habitation,

where my eye,

surprised, perceives in wonder

a more magic reversal: turned around

in backward winds,

it's become its original, own ghost-tree.

The Mangroves

1

The mangroves move on loops into the tide.

If a dance, it is the sea's illusion,

Her whirled moon around mere rootedness,

And not the movement of giant trees.

For they see nothing in that mingling mirror,

No mock of selves, nor phantom loop on loop,

Nor even, when the brothering tide is dead,

Fright of crabs, or muck of their dim birth.

Sticks they are, of seas's periphery,

Simplest bone or fibre of the storm.

2

Once wind blew them in pointless ecstasy,

Conspiring with the sea, and it with the tide,

Whose mother is the moon: these saltiest trees

Made of muck strange twinings in the eye.

Leaved of ships, they rigged the sheller's shore

With sticks and stars of voyages

That shell portended to the seaward eye.

They had their only being in the eye

Which longed to see something of itself

In that distance, or their ivoried stride.

Mangrove

3

And so the walker brings to swamp disorder,

Yet order too, for possibilities

Cannot be had among the mangrove selves,

However they twist by sea in thickest beauty,

Charming him, who for that there walks:

This is as certain as that the empty page

Requires a beast of time, a surly ego,

Pushing his fool against the cramping margin

To bring the page the tale it meant to frame.

It is the stormy walker sets them free.

The Pine

1

Pines stand straight in thin austerity,

Over starred palmetto, lizard-tangle, shrub,

Fingers against burning sky

Perfectly vertical in the flat land.

Bark scaled in the heat like lizard skin,

Sun-sentineling, poem of monotony

Of the tropics, ranged like telephone poles

Across the light-assaulted eye, their

Cones like grenades lying on the dry featherbed

Of needles, where stir the scorpion

And beetle, where crawl in their old kingdoms

Grass snake and coral. In the hammocks,

Yearning for sea, and out by the sea,

Mangroves twist and twine,

Miming the deep movement of water,

Saltstung in grandeur, but it is the tall pine

Which speaks of our land, chaste in the blaze

That burns us to bone.

2

My brother and I wandered

Palmetto and Pine

In the sumptuous thicket,

Stick in hand

To kill a snake:

The pine blossoms

Spiked the white sky

And the wind whished

In the leaves, while

Centipedes curlicued

The cool sand underfoot:

Sudden shriek of birdvoice

And the long haunt of light

Led us to dusk:

We stood listening

And then, scrambling like lizards,

Caught a green snake

And brought it home curled

On our handlebars

3

You cannot climb a pine. The palm,

In its dream of the East, curves to your will.

Now the palms are departing.

The banyan, winding around its memory,

Lies in suburban pockets. The mangrove

Dissolves into the sea.

Inland, across the hot land, the pine,

Rumorous in the air, lifts its thin stars of needles,

While the ancient scorpion waits beneath.

The House of Stone
and Branch

1

Once he thought

That coral and pine

Were the gnarled stuff

From which he might build

His tropical house,

An architecture of light

Sprung from the ground.

Seasoil and salt grape

And the skysweet mango

Would blossom there

Under his hands,

Among the quick lizards

And slow scorpions.

He thought to raise high

A private green arbor,

Aspiring in the pines

Over somnolent sumps,

A house tall as the pines,

Its foundation deep,

Like a vine trailing upward

Carrying moss,

Or a frog in the water,

Eyes bulged at the sun.

There, rock walls would let in

Viridian light, bringing

Into his rooms

The aquatic shadows

Of palms and birds.

Such a house of stone

And branch, enfolding

Anemone,

Twining to herons,

Of the breathing of coral.

The lifting of pine,

Was the dream of his hands.

2

But the time has washed past,

Having its way:

Belly up, the fish glide

Into the Gulf

With misted eyes, and the sun

Burns down on withering

Palm, scorpion husk.

Banyan and mangrove

Have slipped their old roots,

While coral hardens

And crumbles

In the grim suburbs,

Trimming prim cactus;

And those hands

That envisioned

The piling of stone,

The carving of pine,

Are clenched with the years.

Yet sometimes now,

Where the lizards

Still enter

And flick through his porch

And the peacock screams

In its hedge down the street,

He can see

The tall shape,

With the swamp birds circling

Its salty towers

And the turtles crawling toward it

From the sea,

And that submarine sheen,

That skyward light,

Rising up, dazzling,

From hammock and grove,

Over the land.

The Sandflats

(St. Petersburg, 1935)

1

Palmetto thickets, snake-

Whispering brush,

Pine, needle-carpets cool after

Sand-blaze under toes,

Where we tread cautiously

Avoiding stickers

(Which all hurt,

Dried, baked, or weathered,

But especially the green ones

Under the raw toes

Or the balls of the feet

Bit:

We hopped with sudden cry:

A quick yank:

Pinpoint of blood)

And the lunar sandflats,

Swampsmelly, slimepuddled reaches

But cool play for toedigging,

Florida Oak

Heelscuffing, and, with luck,

Great snakes waiting like omens

On their hot stones

In the white light:

But mostly

Only small crabs askitter

2

The miniature schooltrain

Could be heard

Miles away in the pines

Drumming the ground

(In our ears on the rails)

Where we waited

Lunchbags in hand,

To be instructed

Beyond all this greenery

In the pineboard schoolhouse:

Though in those days

The pines soughed in the windows

And there was the clear call

Of hammocking birds

Under the sky

3

One lunchtime the boys

Took the boy Ned

And held him in a thicket,

While his foolbrother Tom

Looked everywhere:

Then (while we watched)

They said Ned was dead,

And in the high ceremony

Of posturing children,

Spaded behind a dark bush,

While Tom looked on:

With overdrawn gestures

They dug and they dug,

Chanting Ned is dead,

Poor Ned is dead,

And old Tom cried,

And we were afraid

And joined in the chant

4

That Sunday

On the flats

When we walked out,

The dread scorpion came,

Abrupt in the eye,

Pine-needle colored

(Most feared in our hearts

Though corals

Were warned of).

Moving slowly

In carved-out segments,

Architectonic,

He carried curled

His thorned tail

Like an upraised Christ

In a village procession,

Bringing strong poison

Of mortality

And we teased, and we

Crushed him

Under a rock

Poetry Published with Author's Illustrations

"Serena's Speaker," seven poems and one drawing, Pandanus Press, Miami, 1957.

"The Tarot," eleven drawings and eleven poems, *Spirit,* vol. XLVI, no. 2, Fall/Winter 1978-79.

"Dune Pine," one etching, *The Carrell,* vol. 22, 1984.

Cover and two drawings, *The Carrell,* 1984.

"Seeing," cover and six linocut drawings, *Palmetto Review,* No. 3, 1984

"Keaton," *Illuminations,* Spring 1985.

"The Shell," "The Sea," and two linocut illustrations, *The Carrell,* Fall 1985.

"The Tarot," twenty-two drawings and twenty-two poems, *Spirit,* 1985.

"Talisman," "Winds," "After Many Years," "Late Light," "Two Young Poets at Night," "The Arrival," *Spirit,* vol. LII, 1986.

Illustration for "Birdman" (ink), *Albatross,* vol. 1, issue 2, 1986.

"Poem on an Empty Page," "Birdman," ink drawing, *Albatross,* vol. 1, issue 2, 1987.

"Etching the Sea Grape Tree," *Montana Review, vol.* 9, Summer 1987.

"Echo," cover and three etchings, *The Carrell,* vol. 25, 1987.

"Perhaps," *Boulevard,* Fall 1987.

"The Solar Heater Plant," "The Pine," illustration and cover print, *Spirit,* Spring 1988.

"Dog Island" (as a poem in progress), and illustration, *The Carrell,* vol. 27, 1989.

Illustrations to Accompany Other Published Literary Works

Frontispiece for *Ceremonies in Mind,* poems by Tram Combs, St. Thomas, 1959.

Drawing, *Inland* magazine, Denver 1961.

Ten ink illustrations, *Voyages from Troy,* poems by Ronald Perry, Mariner Press, Miami, Florida, 1962.

Two graphics, *Spirit,* vol. XXXVI, no. 3, Fall 1969.

Ink drawing, *Spirit,* vol. XXXVII, no. 1, Spring 1970.

Four etchings, *Florida Quarterly,* vol. IV, no. 3, Winter 1972.

Five drawings, *Nijinsky,* a poem by Glory Grasmuck, Jaguar Press, Miami, Spring 1975.

Two prints, *Spirit,* Fall/Winter 1978.

Five drawings, *En Passant,* no. 8, 1979.

Four drawings, *En Passant,* no. 10, 1980.

Cover drawing, *The Riddles of Finnegans Wake,* by Patrick McCarthy, Fairleigh Dickinson University Press, 1980.

Covers for *Spirit,* 1974–1980.

Cover, Program, Third International Conference on the Fantastic in the Arts, March 10–13, 1981.

Frontispiece drawing, *Olaf Stapledon,* by Patrick McCarthy, Twayne Publishers, Boston 1982.

Cover and three illustrations, *The Carrell,* University of Miami Library, 1983.

Cover drawing, "Tremayne," four poems by Donald Justice, *The Windhover Press,* Iowa City, 1984.

Cover illustration, *The Carrell,* vol. 24, 1986.

Cover illustration, three interior etchings, *The Carrell,* vol. 25, 1987.

Back and front cover and three interior prints, *The Carrell,* vol. 26, 1988.

Illustrations for *The City of the Sandalwood Forest* (Tales from the Laostian), by Ronald Perry.

Three ink drawings for Ronald Perry's "Laotian Tale," chapbooks, Philadelphia.

Cover print for Charles Willeford's *Cockfighter,* Neville Publishing, Inc. Santa Barbara, California, 1989.

Art Exhibitions

Mirell Gallery, Coconut Grove, Florida, group shows, 1959, 1960, 1963.

Natalie Baskin Gallery, Coconut Grove, Florida, award show, 1959; one-man show, 1960.

Village Corner Gallery, Miami, Florida, one-man shows, 1961, 1962.

Miami Beach Art Center, Florida, one-man show, 1962.

Key West Art Center, Florida, one-man show, 1963.

Beth Sholem Temple, Miami Beach, Florida, group show, October 1963; one-man shows 1962, 1963, 1965, 1967, 1978.

Hortt Memorial Show, Fort Lauderdale Art Center, Florida, 5th annual 1963, 6th annual 1964, 7th annual 1965.

Sindelir Gallery, Coconut Grove, Florida, one-man show, March 1964.

First Annual Drawing Exhibition, Fort Lauderdale Art Center, Florida, 1964.

The Gallery, Morgan town, West Virginia, one-man shows 1964, 1965.

LeHigh Acres, All-Florida Annual Fiesta, January 1965.

Contempora Gallery, Fort Lauderdale, Florida, one-man show, March 1965.

Artist's Equity Group Show, Bacardi Building, Miami, Florida, September 1965.

Artist's Equity Group Show, Bass Museum, Miami Beach, Florida, October 1965.

Florida Memorial University Group Show, November 1965.

Lowe Art Museum, University of Miami, one-man show 1965.

Art Center, St. Simon's Island, Georgia, one-man shows 1966, 1967.

Baker Gallery, Coconut Grove, Florida, one-man shows 1967, 1968, 1969.

Sanford Museum, Cherokee, Iowa, one-man show, July 1968.

Miami Art Center, Florida, Memberships Exhibition, September 1969.

Invitational Art Exhibit, Museum of Science and History, Miami, Florida, 1969, 1970, 1971, 1972, 1973, 1974, 1976, 1979, 1980, 1981.

Longboat Key Art Center, Sarasota, Florida, one-man show, February 1970.

Washington Federal, Miami Beach, Florida, one-man show, March 1970.

Clemmer Galleries, Coconut Grove, Florida, groups show, January 1971.

International Student Union, University of Miami, Florida, one-man show, February 1971, October 1975.

Temple Beth Am, Miami, Florida, one-man show, October 1975.

New and Retrospective (170 prints and drawings) one-man, Miami Public Library, under auspices of Dade Council of Arts and Sciences, in cooperation with Dade County Library and Roberta Daves of Yesterday's Child art gallery, December 1980.

The Galleries, West Palm Beach, two-man exhibit, April 16–May 15, 2000.

Awards

First Prize, Natalie Baskin Award, Natalie Baskin Gallery, Coconut Grove, 1959.

Honorable Mention, Hortt Memorial Show, Fort Lauderdale Art Center, 1964.

Honorable Mention, LeHigh Acres All-Florida Fiesta, 1965.

Five ink drawings and a woodcut print on commission to Metro, to be issued instead of keys to the city, 220 of each piece lithographed, 1974.

Four drawings in *Born of the Sun,* the Official Bicentennial Commemorative Book of Florida, 1976.

Barker Collection, Lowe Art Museum, University of Miami.

Laurence Donovan, poet and graphic artist, was born in Vancouver, B. C., in 1927 and lived in Florida from the age of ten until his death in 2001. Poet, graphic artist, and teacher, he retired from the University of Miami, where he taught courses in contemporary and ancient literature and creative writing. During his thirty-five-year tenure at the University of Miami he edited and illustrated *The Carrell,* a literary magazine, and regularly wrote book reviews for *The Miami Herald.* He published poems and drawings in most of the better little magazines like *The New England Review* and *Boulevard* and was included in the *Borestone Mountain Best Poems of 1968 and 1970,* where he won First Prize. *Donovan's Tarot,* a collection of twenty-two poems and accompanying linocuts, was published by *Spirit Magazine* of Seton Hall. His art has been exhibited widely throughout the country. He illustrated numerous books, including small press chapbooks by such poets as Donald Justice, Tram Combs, and Ronald Perry. More recent chapbook illustrations were for "The St. Kitts Monkey Feuds," a poem by Laurence Lieberman published by Cummington Press in 1995. He also illustrated Lieberman's collection, "Flight from the Mother Stone" (Arkansas, 2000). Donovan exhibited prints in a two-man show at The Galleries in April–May 2000 in West Palm Beach.

If you enjoyed reading this book, here are some other books from Pineapple Press on related topics. For a complete catalog, write to Pineapple Press, P.O. Box 3889, Sarasota, FL 34230 or call 1-800-PINEAPL (746-3275). Or visit our website at www.pineapplepress.com.

Florida in Poetry edited by Jane Anderson Jones and Maurice O'Sullivan. The first comprehensive anthology of Florida poetry that features a cross-section of voices enchanted by, complaining about, wondering at, and disgusted with Florida's environment and character. Includes poems by Walt Whitman, Langston Hughes, and Elizabeth Bishop, among many others. ISBN 1-56164-083-2 (hb)

Art in Florida: 1564–1945 by Maybelle Mann. With more than 150 illustrations culled from public and private collections around the country, this lush book presents the history of art in Florida, from the first European artists to the Modernists, who forged a new frontier in art after World War II. ISBN 1-56164-171-5 (hb)

Art Lover's Guide to Florida by Anne Jeffrey and Aletta Dreller. Tour 86 of the most dynamic and exciting art groupings in Florida, and learn about the distinctive and eccentric personalities connected with the world of art. ISBN 1-56164-144-8 (pb)

Adventuring in Art by Lois Bartlett Tracy. Greatly enriched by 106 art reproductions by famous artists, this instruction book offers over 200 experiments that will improve the technique of any artist, new or experienced. ISBN 0-910923-79-5 (pb)

The Book Lover's Guide to Florida edited by Kevin McCarthy. Learn which authors lived in or wrote about a place in Florida, which books describe a place, and what important movies were made there in this exhaustive survey of writers, books, and literary sites. ISBN 1-56164-012-3 (hb); ISBN 1-56164-021-2 (pb)